Rooted *in* Resilience

QUESTIONS, PROMPTS, AND EXERCISES TO DISCOVER EVERYTHING YOU'RE CAPABLE OF

There are chapters of life that grow us through challenge, and strengthen us through adversity.

We emerge from these chapters as different people... sometimes quite profoundly. And while we may not see it in the moment, we can look back and notice that through these difficulties, we discovered new ways of being. This is not to say we need to be grateful for these times, but it is to say we can be grateful for ourselves and our own incredible capacity.

This journal is a place to recognize and honor the challenges that have shaped you. It is a place to celebrate the strength that has carried you through. And it is a place to recognize and grow the phenomenal capacity within you. When you root deeply into your resilience, your whole world changes too.

Be rooted
in your self

You are your own greatest resource, your own first responder, your own most steadfast ally. This doesn't mean that you need to meet life's work alone... But when you learn to be at rest in yourself and familiar with your own strengths and resources, you can be more at home wherever you are, and with whatever is happening.

...journey home to yourself...

THEMA BRYANT

What does it look like and feel like to be "at home" with and in yourself?

In what ways do you feel more powerful when you are "at home" in yourself?

What are the actions, rituals, movements, and thoughts that return you to your center?

Return to your center.

SYLVIA SALOW

If they hadn't tried to break me down, I wouldn't know that I'm unbreakable.

GABOUREY SIDIBE

There's a core part of you that is potent, defiant, and unbreakable—a part of you that always continues. What does this part of you feel like? How would you describe it? Where does it live in you?

...flexibility...
is a sign of life.

ANTHONY LAWLOR

Flexibility allows for movement, evolution, growth, and change—it gives you the capacity to bounce back. What does flexibility feel like to you? How would you describe it? Where does it live in you?

Celebrate today for wherever you are in the process.

ANGELA HOWELL

It can be easy to focus on the goals we haven't yet reached, the places we haven't yet arrived at, the growth that hasn't yet been achieved. But take this space to notice and celebrate the big things you have already completed, the growth that has already happened, and the progress you have already made.

Some favorite things about the life you live:

Some specific qualities you are proud to have refined:

Deliberate work you put in to arrive where you are today:

May I be kind
to myself in
this moment.
May I give
myself the
compassion
I need.

KRISTIN NEFF

Complete the following statements in a way that feels both kind and true for you.

I'm still learning, and it's okay to ________________________

____.

In the process of changing, I give myself permission to ________

____.

I will not ________________________________
if I don't meet my goals the first time.

I deserve my own immense recognition for ____________

____.

I will show myself compassion even when ____________

____.

How would you describe who you are?

What are you in the process of learning?

What will you no longer do?

What capabilities are you currently exploring?

I know who I am;
I know what I
can and can't do.
I know what I
will and won't do.
I know what
I am capable of...

DOLLY PARTON

...each day I am
more and
more on my
own side.

SUSAN WEISS BERRY

Take a moment to become aware of the back of your body—the back of your head, your neck, your spine, the back of your legs or feet.

Offer yourself a simple phrase: I HAVE MY OWN BACK.

How do your mental and physical states change when you do this?

Build a strong support system

There are people, places, and things in our lives that bring out the best in us. They reflect our strength in moments when we have forgotten it... or they remind us of the ways we have persevered before... or connect us with a sense of potential... or ignite our own deep fierceness. Let these things be a root system for you—constantly strengthening and increasing your capacity to do the things you need to do.

The things
that we love
tell us what
we are.

THOMAS AQUINAS

A "resource" is anything that brings you a strong positive feeling—a sense of comfort, joy, connection... It's a support, no matter what's happening in your life.

Some rituals or routines that are resources for you:

Some physical activities or poses that are resources for you:

Some thoughts that are resources for you:

Some objects that are resources for you:

Tap into these personal resources whenever you're feeling depleted, or rely on them even before things get difficult, to offer yourself preemptive care.

When you leave
a beautiful place,
you carry it with
you wherever
you go.

ALEXANDRA STODDARD

Somewhere in the world is a place that lights you up—a place that comforts and sustains you, relaxes and reinvigorates you.

Start by describing it here. What do you see, hear, touch, smell, taste when you are there?

Now, describe the parts, aspects, and attributes of yourself that feel most alive in this place:

Let this place be with you whenever you need it. Let it connect you to yourself, and to your own deep well of resilience.

Use this space to name the people who bring out the best in you, and the personal strengths and qualities that they connect you to.

Person: ______________________________

Connects me to my: ______________________________

____

____

Person: ______________________________

Connects me to my: ______________________________

____

____

Person: ______________________________

Connects me to my: ______________________________

____

____

A true friend knows your weaknesses but shows you your strengths...

WILLIAM ARTHUR WARD

You are not alone and never will be...

ABDI NAZEMIAN

We each have a collection of beliefs that sustain us—whether they come from our family or culture, our religion or spirituality, or another deeply personal and unique aspect of our selves or our life experiences. What are the beliefs you hold that help you to feel that you are deeply supported and never alone?

Within you, there is a stillness and sanctuary to which you can retreat at any time...

— HERMANN HESSE

When you feel wired, frantic, buzzy, or anxious, what helps you to slow down, access a sense of calmness, or find stillness and sanctuary?

...awake to the
aliveness of
this moment.

ECKHART TOLLE

When you feel foggy headed, drained, or disconnected, what helps connect you to the moment, boost your energy, or be more present?

Offer yourself the gift of your own recognition whenever you meet a personal challenge, navigate through a difficult moment, or rise to the occasion. Celebrate your growth and progress with one or more of the following.

A celebratory song to listen to:

____

A statement of recognition to offer yourself:

____

____

A treat to make or buy:

____

____

A ritual or routine to try:

____

____

Today, I recognize and celebrate my progress.

AMY E. DEAN

Learn from what has shaped you

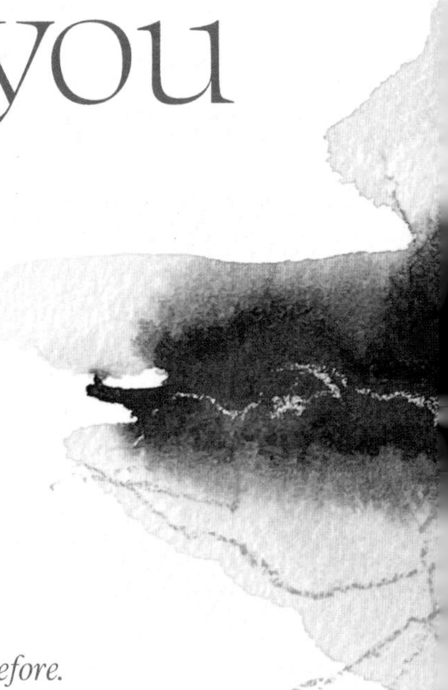

One of the most beautiful aspects of growing in resilience is a deeper sense of belief—not just in the world, but in our selves. We know we will make it through what is happening today because we have made it through difficulty before. By recognizing all we have already overcome, we gain more and more faith in our own strength.

Be faithful to
that which exists
within yourself.

ANDRÉ GIDE

Your unique strengths and abilities create a blueprint for what your particular kind of resilience looks like. Which of the terms below resonate most deeply with you? Use the blank spaces to write in your own.

- ○ *Adaptable*
- ○ *Ambitious*
- ○ *Attentive*
- ○ *Calm*
- ○ *Confident*
- ○ *Cooperative*
- ○ *Creative*
- ○ *Decisive*
- ○ *Diligent*
- ○ *Determined*
- ○ *Direct*
- ○ *Driven*
- ○ *Dynamic*
- ○ *Easygoing*
- ○ *Efficient*
- ○ *Enthusiastic*
- ○ *Gentle*
- ○ *Hardworking*
- ○ *Knowledgeable*
- ○ *Quick-thinking*
- ○ *Receptive*
- ○ *Responsible*
- ○ *Self-assured*
- ○ *Sensitive*
- ○ *Sincere*
- ○ ______________________
- ______________________
- ______________________

What do you love about the way these strengths combine to make you unique?

____

____

____

Think back over the course of your life and take a few minutes to celebrate the effort it has taken you to get this far—all of the times you have tried. *From learning to read to learning to make your way in the world, from learning to move on after a setback to learning to advocate for yourself, there are thousands of times you have stretched yourself in a new direction, grown a new skill, or worked to achieve something.*

Use this space to list as many things as you can.
They can be as small or as big as you like...

Great things happen to those who don't stop believing, trying, learning...

ROY T. BENNETT

...we are stronger, gentler, more resilient, and more beautiful than we imagine...

MARK NEPO

In what ways are you stronger than you tend to recognize or give yourself credit for?

In what ways are you gentler than you might honor or acknowledge?

...we... have the capacity to invent our lives, to shape our destinies in ways that maximize our well-being.

BELL HOOKS

Once we've passed a particularly challenging chapter in our lives, it can be surprising to look back and realize that the thing we were struggling with so deeply is something we have now grown beyond. Seeing this is a powerful reminder that we are wiser now than we've ever been... and that we are still and always evolving.

Think back to a past moment when you were working through something that has now been resolved. What was the challenge or issue?

What do you want to tell your past self about the skills and qualities that carried you through?

What do you suspect your future self might tell you about the things that will carry you through the current chapter of your life?

I can be changed by what happens to me. But I refuse to be reduced by it.

MAYA ANGELOU

Think back to a recent difficult time. What are the ways that this time made you more*—more steady, more capable, more steadfast, more skilled, more whole, or more deeply yourself?*

What are some of the recent moments in your life that have grown your sense of courage?

We don't develop courage by being happy every day. We develop it by surviving difficult times and challenging adversity.

BARBARA DE ANGELIS

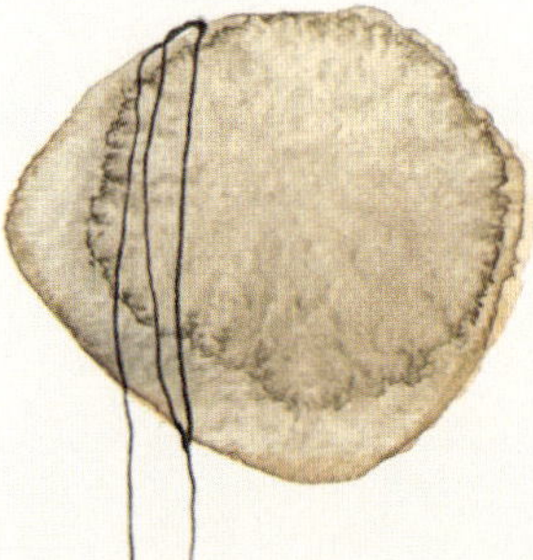

All you can do
is all you can do,
but all you can
do is enough.

ARTHUR L. WILLIAMS JR.

What skills and tools have you used in past challenging situations, even if they aren't the skills and tools you would use today?

What skills and tools have you gained since then?

Work with what's already here

Resilience-building opportunities don't have to be huge or out of the ordinary to be meaningful. There's room for growth in the smaller places too—all the little daily tasks and challenges. Our days are full of chances to practice stretching ourselves. Over time, we become more and more able to leave our comfort zone and then, when we're ready, return back "home."

Initiating a conversation, working through a to-do list, keeping a promise we made to ourselves, even running errands can be a chance to develop more strength, capacity, and self-mastery... and a way to grow ourselves daily.

What are three small, ordinary tasks that you'd like to recognize as opportunities for you to grow in resilience?

1. ______________________________

____

____

2. ______________________________

____

____

3. ______________________________

____

____

...may the moment find you eager and unafraid...

HOWARD THURMAN

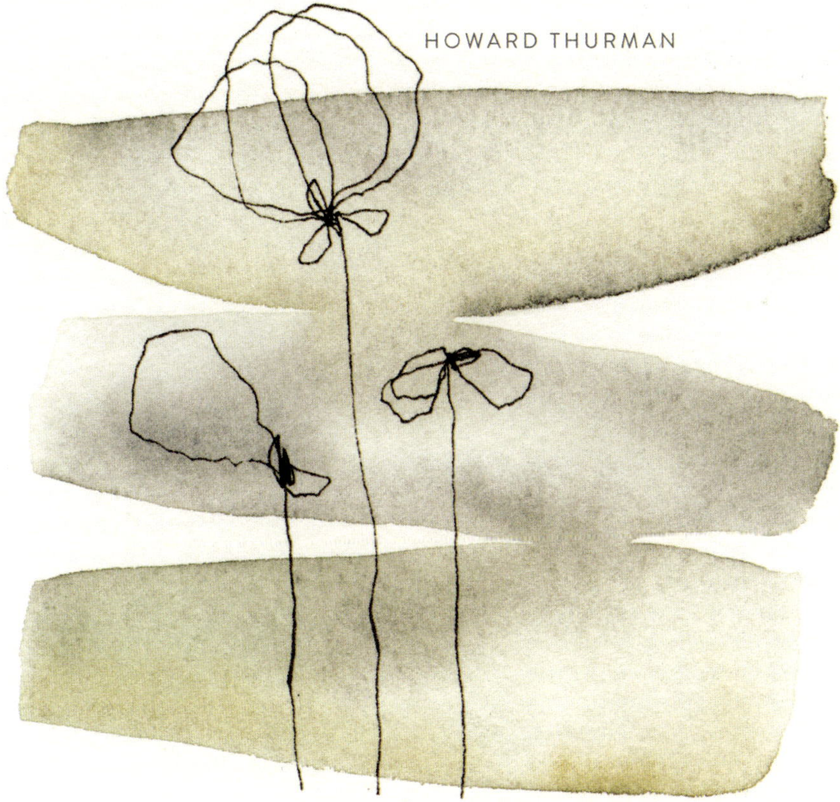

Life won't always be perfect, but there will always be perfect moments if you let them in.

MEGAN HINE

A "glimmer" is a particularly wonderful moment in time—an instant in which you feel a deep sense of joy, safety, peace, or connection. From sweet text exchanges to special breakfasts, a sunny afternoon in the park to a perfect shower before bed, use the space below to create your own glimmer library. How does focusing on glimmers change your sense of well-being?

Your life journey
is about learning
to become more
of who you are
and fulfilling the
highest, truest
expression
of yourself as a
human being.

OPRAH WINFREY

From big stretches to daily tasks, challenges are easier to weather when we know our why*—the reason we're invested in doing the work to begin with. Creativity, family, emotional growth, self-expression, inner healing, financial security, community service, personal fulfillment... The things that motivate us are as individual as we are.*

What matters to you most deeply?

What are the whys *that guide your important choices and decisions?*

What are some tasks and responsibilities you can recognize as smaller parts of bigger things that are deeply important to you?

Dare to be brave today...

MARY DEMUTH

Opportunities for bravery come in all different sizes. Bravery can be engaging in a difficult conversation, speaking your truth, taking a new risk, being more visible, trying something new, asking for something different...

What are some brave actions you are currently taking?

What is a kind of bravery that you are feeling more and more comfortable with?

A moment of radical acceptance is a moment of genuine freedom.

TARA BRACH

What is a situation, whether past or present, that you would like to accept more fully?

Take some time to experiment with the idea *of accepting. What might accepting this situation look like or feel like?*

If you were able to access a greater feeling of acceptance, what do you imagine might change?

You can repeat this process if you like. Notice if and when your feelings soften. Be as slow and gentle with yourself as you need.

What are a few thoughts or concerns that are currently disrupting your personal peace?

Which of these can be safely shelved for a little while until you have more information, time, or clarity?

Choose your thoughts carefully. Keep what brings you peace.

NISHAN PANWAR

Life doesn't get easier
or more forgiving,
we get stronger and
more resilient.

STEVE MARABOLI

What are some things you do regularly these days that used to challenge you?

What are some situations you feel yourself becoming more and more comfortable with?

What's something you can feel yourself becoming strong enough to face?

Create your future

The growth that's happening here is an evolution of you. Your voice strengthens. You speak your truth. You have new confidence and follow-through. And when you are able to love an aspect of a challenge (even if you don't love the whole thing), you are able to rise and meet the world in new ways.

Be kind to yourself as you proceed along this journey.

TSOKNYI RINPOCHE

Put a hand over your heart or chest, or one hand on the opposite forearm. Now, offer yourself a statement that feels good, right, helpful, and true. Try each of the statements below, then create your own.

I'M GETTING BETTER AT THIS.

I AM EQUIPPED TO HANDLE THIS SITUATION.

I TRUST MYSELF TO FIND A SOLUTION.

I CAN BE STEADY IN THIS MOMENT.

I BELIEVE IN MY CAPACITY.

EVEN THOUGH THIS IS CHALLENGING, I WILL BE OKAY.

What are some worthwhile challenges in your life right now—ones that are encouraging you to grow, stretch, and evolve in ways you appreciate? What positive impact does each of these challenges bring?

Challenge: ______________________________

____

The positive impact: ______________________________

____

____

Challenge: ______________________________

____

The positive impact: ______________________________

____

____

Challenge: ______________________________

____

The positive impact: ______________________________

____

____

I love the challenge.

NANCY LOPEZ

The most difficult thing is the decision to act!

AMELIA EARHART

Instead of dreading or putting off the day's most challenging task, think of it as a high-dive moment—a chance to get to the top of the ladder, walk to the edge, count down, and leap!

What are some potential high-dive moments for this week?

Which one will you start with today?

You do not need to know precisely what is happening, or exactly where it is all going. What you need is to recognize the possibilities and challenges offered by the present moment, and to embrace them with courage, faith, and hope.

THOMAS MERTON

What's a situation you currently have some confusion, anxiety, or ambivalence about?

What are some of the possibilities for growth and change you see in this situation?

What do you know about your own capacity that allows you to move forward?

Sometimes knowing what to do is knowing when to stop.

BILL CRAWFORD

What are some instances in your life, whether big or small, when you grew by ending something or stopping your participation?

Is there anything in your life right now that you are considering stopping, ending, or leaving?

What are your own personal ways of knowing when something is no longer worth continuing?

Resilience
means you
experience,
you feel,
you fail,
you hurt.
You fall. But, you
keep going.

YASMIN MOGAHED

As you've worked through the exercises in this journal so far, you've come to a deeper understanding of what resilience means and looks like for you. This is a place to come up with your own definition and explanation.

To me, resilience means:

Keeping going looks like:

COMPENDIUM®
live inspired

Written by: M.H. Clark
Illustrated by: Céline Nordenhed
Edited by: Amelia Riedler
Art Directed by: Steve Potter

ISBN: 978-1-957891-50-7

1st printing. Printed in China with soy inks on FSC®-Mix certified paper.